# ALL THINGS GIRL

## Mind Your Manners

**TERESA TOMEO
MOLLY MILLER
MONICA COPS**

© 2008 by Teresa Tomeo, Molly Miller, and Monica Cops

The "All Things Girl" series is published by
Bezalel Books
Waterford, MI
www.BezalelBooks.com

All titles in the ALL THINGS GIRL series:
*Friends, Boys, and Getting Along*
*Mirror, Mirror on the Wall...What is Beauty After All?*
*Girls Rock!*
*Mind Your Manners*
*Modern and Modest*
*Journal for Prayers, Thoughts, and Other Important Things*

Printed in the United States of America. All rights reserved. No part of this publication may be reproduced, stored in a retrieval system, or transmitted in any form or by any means-for example, electronic, photocopy, recording-without the prior written permission of the author. The only exception is brief
quotations in printed reviews.

References to the Catechism of the Catholic Church are denoted: CCC

ISBN 978-0-9818854-4-5
Library of Congress Control Number 2008931736

This book is dedicated to my family especially my husband Steve, and to all who read the All Things Girl books. You are in my prayers. Ben, Lucy, and Thaddeus, I desperately hope that my attempts at teaching you to chew with your mouth closed, keep your elbows off the table, not talking with your mouth full, etc... will stick! More importantly, I pray that you strive to know, love and serve God and spend eternity with Him.
Love Mom

To my husband Tom, and to my children Patrick, Mark, Gregory, Michael, Elena and Adriana; Thanks for all your love and support!
Mom
And always remember... Mind Your Manners!

To the good Sisters of St. Joseph and my lay grade school teachers at St. Joan of Arc in metro-Detroit who helped teach me the importance of minding my manners and practicing the Golden Rule.
Your examples and witness made a difference in my life.
Teresa

---

High Class ... page 4
Take it from Teresa ... page 9
Mind Your Manners ... page 13
Flowers 101 ... page 18
Girl Talk ... page 26
Five Course Meal ... page 29
Table Manners Quiz ... page 33
Going to see the King ... page 39
Etiquette around the World ... page 43
Autograph Book ... page 48
Tea Time ... page 52
Virtues ... page 54
Girls Gotta Have a Plan ... page 58
St. Faustina ... page 61

## High Class

All people begin life in their mother's womb. From the beginning of your creation, tiny as you were, you were a person. Being created a person, and not, let's say, a kitty or a dog, is special because God gave you a soul that will live forever. A person is a creature made up of a body and a soul. As a person, you are in a "higher class" because your soul is what gives you "the image and likeness of God". Your Creator, God the Father has stamped on your soul, dignity. What is dignity? It is your worth as a person.

## Dignity has three characteristics:

1) You have it no matter what circumstances you live in.
2) You have it no matter what you look like.
3) You have it, no matter what changes you go through in your life.

## *Here are some examples of dignity...*

Jennifer lives in a neighborhood where the houses are very small and the people work hard but don't have much money. Katie lives in a mansion and takes expensive vacations every year. *Which person has more dignity?*

Jade is from Africa and has deep brown skin. Julie has red hair and freckles. Laura is chubby. Maggie is tall and skinny. *Which girl has more dignity?*

Opal is 95 years old and lives in a nursing home and has to be spoon fed. Riley was in a car accident and has a huge scar on her face. Jessica is a beautiful movie star. *Which person has more dignity?*

---

*Hopefully you answered "neither" to all of the examples because all people are equal in dignity. You will go through good and bad times, happiness and sadness, success and failure in your life. Sometimes people think these things are what define you. This is a lie you must not believe.*

*At this point you should be feeling pretty good about yourself.*

*Just in case you need more, check it out, it gets better!*

---

*Always remember...
Your dignity is
a precious gift from God!*

## Princess

When you were a baby, your mom and dad brought you to church to be baptized. What does baptism do? It washes away original sin, makes you a child of God and fills your soul with grace. God is the King of the universe, and you are His daughter: that makes you a princess! As a princess in the royal family of God, you have a value greater than a rare jewel and He loves you soooooo much. This is what defines you as a person and nothing, including popularity, good grades, designer clothes or money, makes a difference in who you are in the sight of God your Father.

So you see, you are so much more than body parts. You are intelligent, creative and caring. You are not an object, but a person, and a female person at that! Sexuality is what makes you a girl, different from males. Only a woman can carry another living person within her body. God also gave to women unique gifts such as a nurturing heart, a giving spirit, and a detail oriented mind. These gifts are used for the good of those around you and for your own true happiness.

Lots of girls grow up trying to answer the soul searching question of *"Why am I here?"*

The answer is simple; *To know, love, and serve God in this life and to be happy with Him forever in Heaven in the next.*

You get to *know, love and serve God from Jesus Christ, the Son of God, who teaches us through the Catholic Church.*

But how do you do all these? Let's go step by step:

### 1. To know God:
What would you do if you want to get to know a movie star? You'd try to read up all the information about him or her in magazines and books, you would watch interviews on TV, ask people around you what they know, etc. Well, you get to know God in a similar way: reading the Bible, listening to your parents talk about God, listening in religion class seriously, praying and receiving the Sacraments.

### 2. To love God:
Did you ever notice that when you have a really good friend you want to spend more and more time with her? And then, the more time you spend with her the more you love her? It's the same way with God. To love God, you need to spend time with Him in prayer, adoring and thanking Him for your blessings, and worshipping Him at Sunday Mass. The amazing thing is, just like with a good friend, the more time you spend with God the more you will love Him!

### 3. To Serve God:
You serve God by serving other people. Serving God is doing daily chores cheerfully without complaining. You serve God when you serve other people through your kind words and compassionate ways. You serve God when you participate in community service projects or do things like visit residents in a nursing home. God is in each and every person so when you serve other people, you are serving God!

**As you grow up, ask Our Lord in what special way He wants you to know, love and serve Him. This will be your vocation and will make you truly happy in your life.**

    Hey girls, it's great to have friends to talk to isn't it? We all love communicating with those we are close to in order to share our thoughts and dreams, or maybe just to catch up or chat about what's going on in our lives. But think about this; imagine what it would feel like if you were having a heartfelt conversation with one of your closest buddies and then in the middle of that conversation that friend whom you thought was really interested in what you had to say, starts talking to someone else? Not only would you think she was rude and inconsiderate but you would probably be hurt and made to feel as if what you had to say wasn't all that important.

    Has this ever happened to you? Well it has happened to me. I remember one very uncomfortable situation several years ago when I was working at a local radio station and speaking with a friend and co-worker. I was recently married at the time and she was asking me about my wedding. As a new bride I was eager to talk about the details; the beautiful wedding Mass at my local parish, the reception, all the family who came to town for the big occasion and of course my new husband. As I started to answer her questions, another station employee came walking toward the newsroom. I was in the middle of a sentence when this young woman simply turned away and started to engage the other person in a conversation about a work related matter. I was stunned. But the experience taught me something about the importance of minding our manners.

This very uncomfortable incident comes to mind often lately, not because I have not forgiven my friend and former co-worker; but because society is seeing more of this rude behavior. Sadly, too many people are now paying more attention to their latest text messages and phone calls than they are to the relative or friend who may be sitting right next to them! It seems that personal, one-on-one communication has gone out the window. It's being replaced by instant messaging, and an entire new language of text messaging that often contains unflattering terms, abbreviations, and incomplete sentences that barely resemble the English language. The latest in technology has, unfortunately, brought with it some very bad habits that are quickly leading to manners becoming a thing of the past.

How bad has the situation gotten? Well, could you imagine working on your lap top during Mass or talking on the cell phone on the way to receive Jesus in Holy Communion? Or how about taking or making a phone call while sitting in the front row during a presentation? All of these cases are true. I've either witnessed them personally or have been told about them by my radio show listeners or some of my acquaintances.

This doesn't mean that technology is all bad. As a matter of fact, the Catholic Church **does not say** that we should throw the computers, cell phones, or TV's, or i-pods out the window. Pope Benedict XVI and the late John Paul II stated many times that the media offers a way for God's people to connect around the globe. They also encourage Christians to use the media to spread the Gospel through such avenues as Catholic radio, Catholic TV, and Catholic web sites. These are the ways in which technology is awesome.

But the Church also warns us that this same technology which opens up major lines of communication and brings the world, literally, to our fingertips can also cause isolation. Just think about that for a minute. When you use too much technology you are really by yourself. God's creatures were made to be in relationship; first with the Lord and then with each other. The statements from our Holy Father given to college students at the University of Parma in 2008 provide all of us with some wonderful words of wisdom about how we need to have a balance; a balance that will not only help us be polite and kind but a balance with the new technology that will also greatly benefit our relationships.

"On the one hand, they run the risk of a growing reduction in their capacity for concentration and mental application on an individual level; on the other, that of isolating themselves individually in an increasingly virtual reality. In doing so, students close themselves off to "constructive relations with others."

Maybe you're reading this right now and saying, "Well, I am not that bad." But if you're like most young people, you probably spend more time with technology than you think. According to Nielsen Mobile, teens 13 to 17 send or receive close to 1,800 text messages per month. Other studies show those most likely to text message are between the ages of 13 and 24. Ask your parents for the exact numbers. It should be on the bill. Or maybe it is already something that you fight about with them. Come on! Check it out so that you can be using technology the right way and not in isolation.

And what about other forms of technology that may be causing you to throw those manners out the window? The average young person spends nearly 40 hours a week using different forms of media and depending on what you're watching or listening to, your media habits could be numbing you to common courtesies **and** to Godly principles. Most youth spend four hours a day watching TV and almost two hours a day listening to music and at least one hour or more on the computer. That means you are spending more time with media than you do with your family, friends, or on school work.

Chances are you might need to sit down with your parents and maybe even your brothers and sisters and do a media reality check. As a media expert, and based on the research I have done, the impact media is having on society and families proves to me that not all children should be having cell phones or lap tops. In my book *Noise* I point out that all the other experts in the medical and psychological fields agree that computers and TV's should be in the central area of the home where parents can monitor activity. Cell phone use should be very limited and used for emergency situations or communication with family members, and more time should be spent in family based activities such as a board game or reading or taking in a sporting activity. These are activities that will not only strengthen your relationships with your relatives but they are activities much more suited to who you really are; a daughter of the King!

Here are some questions to pose for your family discussion:

- How much time do we spent with the various forms of media?
- Have I ever used any form of media to cheat?
- Do I let the computer, cell phone, text messaging, or TV interfere with my prayer time, family time, school work, or face to face conversations?
- Do I use a cell phone or other forms of technology at inappropriate times and locations such as at the dinner table, in the class room, during Mass?
- Do I use inappropriate language or abbreviations in my e-mails or communications that might be offensive to another person or especially to God?
- Am I using the technology to participate in gossip, name-calling, or bullying?
- Do my media related activities honor God or mock my belief system?
- Do I follow rules set down by my parents when it comes to the time I spend with technology?
- What would Jesus think if He were to look at the e-mails or text messages I may have sent recently?

In today's media saturated cultured it is easy to see how minding our manners can be a real challenge. But just stop and think about how you would feel if someone did to you what my friend did to me years ago? Or maybe a similar situation has happened to you. Or, maybe you've been that rude to someone. Think about that, and as daughters of the King apply what is known as the Golden Rule, the words of the King in Chapter 7 of St. Matthew's Gospel.

*"So whatever you wish that men do to you, do so to them; for this is the law of the prophets."*

# Mind Your Manners

*The* Mandersons are looking forward to the family event of the century. Rich Uncle Jim's daughter, cousin Maria, is getting married in Chicago. Uncle Jim is going all out on the occasion. The wedding is at the cathedral and the dinner and reception at the country club. Everyone is excitedly planning for the strictly formal event.

*Mrs.* Manderson is having her five kids take etiquette classes. Mandy is twelve years old and she could care less about all the fuss. She is not being very cooperative with her classes in manners. She thinks it's all a waste of time.

*Finally* the big day has arrived. The Manderson family is decked out in their new outfits. Even Dad is wearing a tuxedo. Mom is a bit worried about Mandy and her manners but is hoping for the best.

*The* Manderson's are seated in church waiting for the wedding march to begin. Mandy decides she has to leave and use the restroom. The music starts for the procession, and Mandy leaves her pew. As the bridesmaids are coming down the aisle, Mandy is walking toward them and to the horror of everyone present, completely interrupts the procession. By the time Mandy is finished in the bathroom, the beautiful bride starts her entrance. Mandy is in a hurry to reach her seat so she cuts in front of Maria and runs to her pew, totally ruining the bride's entrance.

*In* spite of this, the bride and groom continue to smile and meet at the altar where the Mass begins. Everything is back on track and everyone has forgotten about the mishap during the bride's entrance and is focused on the sacrament taking place in front of them. The first reading is from Song of Songs and is about great love. People are gently dabbing at the tears forming in the corners of their eyes. Mandy only rolls hers, in disgust.

*During* the second reading, Mandy sneezes without covering her mouth and sprays everyone around her. Then, to make matters worse, if that's possible, she wipes her nose with her sleeve. People around Mandy watch in stunned amazement, that a young girl could have such dreadful manners.

*While* the priest is giving his sermon, Mandy answers her cell phone, which she forgot to turn off. In order to be quiet, she decides to text for the rest of the sermon. She gives herself a silent pat-on-the-back for such quick thinking.

*During* the vows, the bride and groom are very emotional and they speak their vows very quietly. Mandy blurts out, "Speak up! I can't hear what you're saying!" After receiving the Precious Blood, Mandy gives a loud hiccup. To make matters worse, Mandy's mother has been trying to get Mandy's attention throughout the ceremony in order to signal her that she should sit with her legs together. Mandy had made herself quite comfortable and was sitting like a truck driver in her nice dress. After the final blessing and exit, Mandy pushes her way through to see her cousin Maria and tell her "Congratulations!" Again giving herself kudos for what she considered to be "proper" behavior. After all, wasn't that what her mom was harping on her about?

*Mrs.* Manderson obviously wasn't as pleased with Mandy as Mandy was with herself. Mrs. Manderon took Mandy aside and begged her to mind her manners. She gives her daughter a few pointers and then prays the rest of the event goes better. Mandy is clueless about her mother's humiliation.

*At* the reception Mandy sees many of her cousins and asks her mother if it would be okay to hang with them. They are all planning to sit together at dinner. Mom gives her approval, hoping that Mandy will act better with peers.

*The* tables are set with fine china, crystal and silver. As the priest says the blessing Mandy asks loudly, "Why do we have so many forks?" The first course is served, followed by salad and then dinner. Mandy is so excited to be with her cousins she is talking a mile a minute with her mouthful. Instead of asking to have the salt and pepper passed, she reaches over the cute boy sitting next to her, getting gravy on her sleeve. Now one of her sleeves has snot on it and the other  has gravy! Oh well, on with the fun. She smiles at him with salad greens stuck between her teeth.

*Mrs.* Manderson and the kids want to get group pictures taken. Mandy has to go to the restroom to freshen up. When she returns for her picture, her dress is stuck in the back of her panties and she is dragging toilet paper under her foot. Mandy's mom gets her daughter put together and the picture taking resumes.

*It's* time for the relatives to meet old friends of the family. Mr. And Mrs., Manderson gather their family to introduce them to Mom's old neighbor, Mrs. Ogden. Each child politely shakes her hand, until Mandy's turn comes. Mandy looks at Mrs. Ogden's outstretched hand and exclaims, "I'm not touching that hand! Look at those big veins! She must be 100 years old!" Mandy then turns and runs away.

*Mandy* hooks up with her cousins and other kids her age. The dance is about to begin. The bride and groom are dancing to their favorite romantic song. Mandy sees that cute boy and runs across the dance floor just about knocking over the lovely couple! Soon all the guests are dancing. Mandy begins shouting to her friends so they can hear her over the music.

*Finally,* the night is over. The Mandersons are getting all the kids ready to go home. Mandy goes to get her coat. She overhears that cute boy tell her cousin that he thought Mandy was the rudest and most selfish girl he'd ever met. Mandy is crushed. How could he say that? What in the world did she do to deserve such an insult?

*Mandy* certainly was not acting the part of a princess. Find all the things Mandy did that were bad manners. See if you caught them all. The answers are on the next page.

*Mandy forgot that her behavior should always reflect that she is a daughter of the King. Don't you forget that important fact!*

## Answers

Mandy...
has a bad attitude about learning manners.
leaves the pew right when the procession is starting and interrupts the bridesmaids.
cuts in front of the bride.
sneezes without covering her mouth.
wipes her nose with her sleeve.
answers her cell phone in church.
text messages in church.
blurts out comments during the vows.
sits in a very unlady-like way.
gives a loud hiccup after Communion.
pushes her way through the crowd to congratulate her cousin.
interrupts the priest during grace.
talks with her mouth full.
reaches over others to get the salt and pepper.
forgets to check her appearance in the bathroom and drags around toilet paper.
makes a rude comment about an elderly woman in front of her.
interrupts the bride and groom on the dance floor.
shouts across the room.

# Flowers 101

Do you remember picking a dandelion when you were a little girl and giving it to your mom? What a smile that simple act of kindness brought to her face! Flowers add so much to our lives! They are given to encourage people, congratulate and even say "I'm sorry." In the home, flowers add a touch of cheerfulness and can complement a decorating style in a room. Flowers are great for centerpieces on your dinner table.

## Caring for cut flowers is easy. Here are some tips on how to make cut-flowers stay fresh longer:

- *Once you have picked flowers from your yard – or brought some home from the store-, it is very important to re-cut the bottom of the stems at an angle. This will create a larger stem area for water to be taken up by the flower. Plunge the stems in water immediately after cutting to prevent air locks.*
- *Remove from the stem the leaves that would be submerged in water. If you don't, they will soon rot, making the water in the vase stale.*

## You may prolong the life of a flower arrangement by:

- *Checking every day the water level and adding water if necessary. Some flowers are "heavy drinkers!"*
- *Change the water completely once a week. Wash the container with hot water and soap before re-filling it. This will get rid of bacteria forming.*
- *Remove any dead or discolored foliage and re-cut stems every four days.*
- *Keep flowers away from heat sources and direct sunlight.*

## Tips for arranging flowers:

- *Begin with the tallest flowers, for example snapdragons. Hold flowers, one at a time, next to the vase you will be arranging. Cut stems so that they're one and a half times taller than the vase. Not all flowers have to be cut the*

*Page 18*

*exact same length. You can give or take and inch. Position flowers in the vase.*

- *Take the second tallest flowers such as gladioli, and again, hold next to the vase; cut stems so that they stand a few inches shorter than the tallest flowers. Position at the front of the vase (in front of the tallest flowers)*
- *Accent the arrangement with other flowers, such as tulips; place these in between the other flowers to harmonize the arrangement.*
- *Flower arrangements can be many colors of flowers put together, or one color in different shades. A cool idea for Mothers Day, for instance is making a flower arrangement for your mom, picking her favorite color and using different shades of flowers together.*

## Potpourri How To's

Potpourri is a perfumed mixture of dried flowers, herbs, seed heads, spices and essential oils. It has been used for centuries as a natural way of sweetening the air or hiding less pleasant aromas. Potpourri also adds a splash of natural color to a room.

## Fun Autumn Potpourri

**Step 1:** The first thing to do is to dry orange peels. Peel 3 oranges and place the peels on a paper plate. Microwave for five minutes at half power, turning peels over halfway through. Let the peels dry for a few days.

**Step 2:** You will need to plan a nature walk in the woods in order to collect the following: pine needles, pinecones, acorn caps, cedar bows and walnuts. You will need to fill half way a brown paper grocery bag. When you get home, if you are not planning to finish making the potpourri right away, you may place your gatherings in large plastic bags, that seal tight, in your freezer for up to 3 weeks.

**Step 3:** Prepare the spices: In a heavy paper bag, mix: 6 cinnamon sticks, 6 whole nutmegs, 2 vanilla beans and ½ cup of cloves. Close the bag and tape shut. Smash ingredients inside the bag with a hammer, until they are turn into tiny pieces but are not powdery. Do this on a surface that can take the smashing hammer!

Step 4: Assemble the potpourri by mixing the dried orange peels, outdoor supplies that you gathered in the woods and smashed spices in a large paper bag. Shake bag to stir up ingredients. Divide potpourri into jars, cool bowls or bags and decorate with ribbon if you are giving these away for gifts.

Enjoy the aroma!

## Sweet Flower Potpourri

Step 1: Collect flowers and herbs from your garden or yard. It's best if you do it in the morning after the dew has dried.

Step 2: Take the petals off the larger flowers, and pick the leaves off the herbs. The smaller flowers you'll want to leave whole. Spread small flowers, petals and leaves on a baking sheet lined with paper towels. Let dry. It'll take several days. Flowers and petals should feel crisp. Some flowers will have a stronger scent than others; You may want to dry flowers that although are not very aromatic, have bright colors, to give the potpourri a more colorful appearance.

Step 3: Mix dry herbs and flowers together. Choose a glass jar or a bowl where you'll want to display your potpourri and place flowers in it. Sprinkle with several drops or teaspoons of your favorite essence such as rose oil, dried lavender, lemon balm or jasmine. When the aroma weakens, add more drops of the blend to re-freshen the aroma.

Step 4: You can make sachets by cutting a 7 inch diameter circle of fabric. Place a few spoonfuls of already scented potpourri in the middle of the circle. Gather the fabric towards the center and tie the bundle with a cool ribbon. Place sachets in your drawers to keep clothes smelling fresh. Sachets also make great gifts!

## Daughters of the King have Manners!

**How** many times have your own parents said, "Mind your manners?" Maybe you have acted like our friend Mandy. Hopefully you have not done all the things she did, especially in one day! But chances are you've done some of them over the course of a few days or week or month.

**So,** what are manners? Manners are not a bunch of random rules to follow, nor are they a long list of no-nos. Manners are much more than that! They are ways to show others that you really care about them. Manners might be a simple "thank-you" note to a friend who bought you a present or holding the door for someone. Manners are putting others first and yourself last. Every person is created in the image and likeness of God; therefore they deserve to be treated with respect. You show your respect for others by the way you greet them, and talk, or interact with them. A young woman with nice manners gets respect because she gives it; she has a lot of confidence in herself.

**Manners** are necessary for people to get along with each other and live in harmony. Imagine a world where nobody respects another, where people do whatever they feel like doing even if it hurts or inconvenience others; Welcome to *Selfishtown*! It takes forgetting about you to acquire good manners.

*Manners* include many aspects of your life, such as greeting people, table manners, and even body posture. Think about how you feel when:

- *Someone sitting across from you at the dinner table eats with his or her mouth open.*
- *A person sitting next to you at dinner reaches across you to get the salt.*
- *You see a girl in a skirt sitting across the room with her legs spread eagle.*
- *A person next to you coughs and sneezes on you.*
- *You are talking with someone and they interrupt you.*
- *When someone lets a door close in your face.*
- *If someone laughs at you (instead of with you).*

*These* things can hurt your feelings, gross you out, or irritate you. God put us on this earth hoping we will be good and kind to one another. Manners are one great way to do just that! Using good manners are acts of kindness. And all acts of kindness make us feel good, too! What a win-win situation.

*Using* manners are a way of letting others know you care about how they feel. And, very importantly, using manners show you realize the beauty and wonder it is being the daughter of the King!

## Let's Have a Word!
**Words, words, words.** They make up your daily communication with others. You use them to greet people, to compliment others, to express your feelings and opinions and even to complain! Words are very important. They can define the outcome of a situation. It is important for you to know that the words you use with your friends at school, may not be the right words to use while talking to some adults at the neighbor's ice-cream social.

## Nice to Meet You!
Meeting new people is great! The way you greet them says a lot about your person. If you are introduced to someone and you are looking down to the ground while shaking their hand means that you don't really care to meet them.

So, what's the proper way to greet somebody new?
- It is important to make eye contact: it shows people that you are honest and that you are interested in them.
- Listen very carefully for the person's name and repeat it as you are being introduced. "Nice to meet you Mrs. Welsch" Repeating the person's name will help you remember it later.
- Shake hands with a firm grip when you are saying hello to an adult.

What about introductions? Here are some situations where you will need to play the role of "Introducer":
- You just arrived at the movie theater with your friend Heather, and there you bump into Sheila, your neighbor.

What do you do? Well, you need to introduce them to each other! "Heather, this is my neighbor, Sheila". "Sheila, this is my friend Heather". It's that easy!
- Your friend Amanda comes to your house for the first time. It is important that you introduce her to your parents right away.

## Attempt Words

*Hmm…Nah…Huh?...Bah!...*We call these "attempt" words because that's what they really are! They are words that have nothing to do with a conversation. We all use "attempt" words here and there. The problem is when they are overused:

Imagine this conversation between friends:
- *Wanna c'me?*
- *Hmm….Nah!*
- *Huh?*
- *Ok, Yeah!*

Who really knows what they were saying! There are situations where the use of "attempt" words is rude, such as talking to any adults like your teachers, a boss, or a parish priest.

## Swear Words and Put Down Words

These words are designed to insult and offend people. Did you know that? They make conversations nasty. Remember that as a Daughter of the King you want to use words that reflect your dignity, your royalty. You want to use words that uplift others, not put them down. Think about the Blessed Mother and imagine how she talked to the people around her. She must have used kind words in her conversations; she complimented people and was kind. That's who you need to imitate!

## To Ask or Not to Ask

It's good to have conversations with adults. It is great to be interested and ask questions. However, there are some things a young person should not ask an adult.

Read the following sentences and decide which ones would be inappropriate to ask and adult:

    a. Your chocolate cake is so good, Mrs. Hunt, could I please have your recipe?
    b. Why can't Beth come over for a sleepover, Mr. Watterfall? Don't you trust my parents?
    c. I love your new purse, Mrs. Jamison, how much did you pay for it?
    d. What a cute puppy, Mr. Landa, can I pet him?
    e. What's the matter with your husband, Mrs. Holland, why is he always sleeping when I come over?
    f. Is that your real hair, Mr. Bauldy? Or is it fake?
    g. Nice necklace, Mrs. Collard, did you make it yourself?

**Don't ask it!**    Answer Key: Inappropriate questions: b, c, e, f

Questions aren't the only things that can be rude sometimes. The statements you make can sometimes come across rather rough or give the impression that you are a show off, or that you have no manners.

Read the following statements and decide which ones would be inappropriate:

    h. My mom spent a lot of money to buy your birthday gift, Amy.
    i. I love ice cream, let's go and have some!
    j. No thanks, Mrs. Beans, I hate broccoli, I don't want any.
    k. I am so excited; I just got a new outfit at the mall! It's so adorable; I can't wait to wear it to show the whole school how cute I look!
    l. Dad, I got the highest grade of the class on math test!
    m. I'm sorry Mrs. Thorn, I'm unable to baby-sit for you on Friday night, I have a volley-ball game.
    n. I hate going to Aunt Gertrude's house, she is so boring!

**Don't say it!**    Answer Key: Inappropriate statements h, j, k, n

# Can We Talk About Girl Talk?

It has been said before and is worth repeating: daughters of the King speak with kindness, compassion, and humility. Everything about them, from their posture to the words they use, should reflect who they are in Jesus. Virtuous speaking means choosing words carefully and with wisdom. Here are a few pointers:

- If you can't say something nice, don't say anything at all.
- Vulgar language is NOT an option.
- Swearing is a NO-NO.
- Dirty jokes are to be avoided. If someone tells one around you either walk away or say something like, " Real nice…," "That's disgusting!" or "Keep it to yourself next time."
- Name-calling is not nice, so don't do it.
- Conversation about personal bodily functions is tacky, so skip it.
- Talking about personal "girl" stuff should be done privately with mom.

As a rule of thumb, if you couldn't say it in front of our Blessed Mother, don't say it. Remember, she's in Heaven and would hear you anyway! One day all will have to give an accounting, before God, of every word that has been said. That should cause some serious hesitation before speaking!

Imagine, every word matters. Did you know that long ago God told Abraham that everyone who cursed Abraham would be cursed and that everyone who blessed Abraham would be blessed? God was saying, "I listen to everything everyone says."

Whatever comes out of the mouth is there forever. It can't be taken back. The tongue can be as sharp as a two edged sword. Don't use it as a weapon and don't use it to lower your dignity as a princess, so toss the toilet talk! You'll be glad you did.

## Dinner is Ready!

Food, food, food. Who doesn't like good food? Food is such an important part in our interaction with others. Food is present when we celebrate important things with our families. Every holiday has a special food tied to it. Whether it is turkey at Thanksgiving, ham at Christmas, or chocolate-fudge cake on your birthday, people gather around the table to spend time together and enjoy a good meal. Food is good! God wants us to use food to nourish our bodies, but also to "bond" with each other.

> Jesus said, "I am the bread of life; whoever comes to me will never hunger, and whoever believes in me will never thirst."
>
> John 6:35

Jesus gave Himself as food, too! When we partake of Communion, we are consuming the body of Christ.

## Table Manners

What makes the perfect meal? Good food, good company, and good manners. Yes, good manners are essential for making mealtime more pleasant for yourself and for others. The way you hold the silverware, drink, chew your food, and interact with others at the table reflects your dignity as a Daughter of the King. Remember, you are a Princess; therefore you need to have "royal" manners at the table. Besides, it's so much fun to learn!

## Setting the table:

Family meals are so very important! Sometimes they are the only time of the day when a family sits together to simply talk or catch up on things.

There are general guidelines for setting the table whether a casual or formal meal. Perhaps your family already uses some of these guidelines; If not, you may ask your mom if it's okay for you to try them; who knows, she may want to start following these guidelines all the time!

- Forks always go to the left of the plate
- Knives always go to the right, next to the plate, with the sharp edge of the blade facing in.
- Spoons always go to the right of the knives
- Glasses are placed a little to the right of the tip of the knife.
- Cup and saucer are placed to the right of the spoons.
- Bread and butter plate is placed above and slightly to the left of the forks.

## Casual Meals:

You will use this setting most of the time at home and casual restaurants, where the food is served all at once. These types of meals are also called Family Style Meals.

## Plan your own Five Course Meal Party!

Whether to celebrate a big Holiday with your family, or simply to have a special time with friends, a Five Course Meal is a great experience.

First, you need to learn what a Five Course Meal is. Like in a book, each part of the book is called a chapter, in a fancy dinner, each part of the dinner is a called a course. At elegant meals, the food is not brought to the table all at once. Instead, each food is brought to the table one course at a time. Once one course is eaten, the respective plate and silverware are removed and the next food is brought. Most elegant meals have five courses. The following are the standard courses: appetizer, soup, salad, main course or entrée and dessert.

## Let's start by learning how to set the table for a Five Course Meal.

Set the table according to the diagram below. When eating use the utensils from outside in towards the plate (for instance: 1 then 2 then 3).

From left to right:
1. Appetizer fork
2. Dinner fork
3. Dessert fork
4. Dinner knife
5. Salad knife
6. Soup spoon

Above the plate: These are the dessert silverware. To the left of the dessert silverware is placed the butter plate with spreader. To the right of the dessert silverware the water and wine glasses are placed.

## *A word about napkins*

Cloth napkins are a must at a fancy meal. Delight your guests with a special folded cloth napkin at their table place setting. There are many different ways in which you can fold a napkin. You can even create your own way. What is important to remember is that they should look elegant and not all jumbled up. They should have clean, crisp lines and creases and may even need to be ironed before you use them. Napkins can make all the difference in how the table looks so have fun!

## *What's for Dinner?*

Okay, now that you know how to set the table, you will need to choose the menu. Talk to your mom about this, she will have great ideas. The recipes don't have to be complicated or fancy. If you choose to do the cooking, you may want to ask an older sister or cousin to help you. Ready to start? You will need to choose an appetizer, soup, salad, entrée and dessert.

Here are the five courses and a few tips on how to eat each!

1. *Appetizer:* These are items like shrimp cocktail, mozzarella sticks, mini-tacos, etc. Use the outermost fork to eat these.

2. *Soup:* Use the outermost spoon to eat your soup. Never hold your spoon the way you hold your toothbrush! Tilt and move the spoon away from you to fill it with soup. Here's a little saying to help you remember, "As a ship goes out to sea. I push my spoon away from me." Then lift the spoon to your mouth as you lean over the bowl. To get that last tasty drop of soup, you must tilt the bowl slightly away from you and moving the spoon away from you, scoop it up. And remember, never slurp your soup!

3. *Salad:* Use the next fork and outermost knife for the salad. Use the knife to cut large pieces of lettuce or

*Page 31*

vegetables, one piece at a time. Don't cut the entire thing into tiny pieces before you eat the first bite.

4. *Main course or entrée:* This could be beef, chicken, fish, pork, etc. Use the large knife and fork for this course. Don't cut more than a few bites at a time.

5. *Dessert:* Sometimes the dessert silverware which consist of a smaller fork and spoon, are placed on the table, above the dinner plate. At other times, it's brought in with the dessert. Some foods require that you use both silverware to eat them; This is a more refined manner. If, for instance, chocolate cake is for dessert, use the fork to hold the cake, and the spoon to cut a bite size piece; Try it at home, you'll find it fun!

## The Five O'Clock Position:

At a fancy dinner, (and you can do this at home all the time as well), it is very important when you are done with each course to place the knife and fork in the five o'clock position, as the picture shows. The reason for the five o'clock position is that in most places the server will remove your plate from the right. If your utensils are in that position, he simply clamps his thumb over the handles and carries your plate away.

Now you are all set to treat your loved ones to a 5 course meal!

## *Table Manners Quiz:*

Let's see how much you know about table manners. Answer each question True or False.

1. You should place your napkin on your lap as soon as you sit down to eat.
2. When you need butter, you take it from the butter dish and place it directly on your bread.
3. You wait for everybody to sit down to start eating your food, except for the cook –usually your mom-, because she may not be ready to sit down yet anyway.
4. In a family style meal, the food is always passed to the right.
5. When helping yourself from the serving platter, it is okay to choose and pick whatever portion you want regardless if it is the one from the bottom of the platter.
6. If for some reason some food platter didn't get to you, it is okay to ask for it.
7. It is okay for you to mix all types of food on your plate, as long as you are the one eating it.
8. You may leave the table as soon as you are finished eating your food, even if others are not finished.
9. If a piece of food gets stuck in your teeth, it is okay to ask to be excused from the table, go to the bathroom and remove it.
10. It is okay to use your fingers to help get some food such as rice and peas onto the fork.
11. As long as you use silverware, it doesn't matter with which hand and how you hold the fork and knife while cutting your steak.

## *Answers:*

1. True. Placing your napkin on your lap is the first thing you do.
2. False. Butter should be taken from the butter dish and placed on your bread and butter plate, if you have one, or on your dinner plate, not directly on your bread!
3. False. Don't start eating until everyone sits down – and that includes whoever did the cooking.
4. True. The food is passed to the right. If you send something the wrong way, two platters are going to end up creating a "traffic jam". If it's a big dish, help the next person by holding it while he serves himself.
5. False. Take the portion nearest you. Leave the serving utensils neatly together on one side of the dish so they don't "drown" in the sauce or gravy.
6. True. It is okay to ask someone to pass you the food as long as you do it politely. "Please pass the rice". Never reach across the table for something, even if you are tempted to do so!
7. False. Don't mix food on your plate unless it's meant to go together. Gravy over mashed potatoes, yes. But green beans and mashed potatoes, no. It may look good to you, but it probably won't to your fellow diners.
8. False. If you are finished eating your dinner before anyone else, join in the conversation until others are finished.
9. True. If some corn on the cob gets stuck between your teeth, you need to get it out, but not in front of everybody sitting at the table!
10. False. Never use your fingers! You can use your knife or a piece of bread to help get the food onto your fork.
11. False. There is a right and wrong way of holding your fork and knife. When you are cutting, the fork should be in your left hand, tines (these are the points on the fork) down, handle cupped in the palm of your hand and pointer finger on the back of the handle pointing at the tines. The knife should be held on your right hand.

## *The Heart of the Home*

Not all the houses are homes. The word house refers to a building, whether built out of wood, brick or any other material. It's a place of habitation for people. A home is much more than that! A home is a place where an individual or a family can rest and take refuge from the world. Many people think of home as a place where they grew up or where they lived, a place that brings back memories or feelings.

**Women are the heart of the home.** They have the ability to transform a house into a home. It is because of her feminine gifts such as attention to detail, intuition and gentleness that a woman can create the environment of a Christian home, like that of the Holy Family. The Blessed Mother is a beautiful example of a homemaker. It doesn't matter whether a woman is married and lives with her husband and children, or single, and lives alone, with a roommate or family member; she is the heart of her home.

> *The Christian family is a communion of persons, a sign and image of the communion of the Father and the Son in the Holy Spirit.*
>
> **CCC#2205**

There are many wonderful examples of women who have answered this vocation in an anointed way. Pope Benedict XVI's sister spent most of her life creating a home filled with love for her brother. John Paul II called this "gift of self" and it is the way in which women are created in the image and likeness of God who gave of Himself through Jesus.

A woman knows how to make others feel comfortable, how to relieve tiredness, and how to cheer others up. These are great gifts! Women show their love for others in the way they care for their home and family. They do so by paying attention to detail. Although you are still young and don't have a home of your own, you can start practicing ways of being the heart of the home.

It is also important for you to honor the ways in which your mother is trying to create a loving and Christian home. Do you help make your home, right now, a warm and loving place?

**Here are some examples of things you can do now and in the future:**

- Place a flower arrangement on your dinning room or living room table. Flowers cheer people up!
- Give special attention when a family member is sick. Try to anticipate their needs. Keep them company.
- When someone has missed dinner with the family, warm up some food and keep him or her company while eating. You can also have a small salad or side dish so that he or she won't feel self-conscious.
- On birthdays, prepare the person's favorite meal or dessert. Surprise them by decorating the house with balloons.
- If a family member is going through a rough time, get a candy bar for them and leave it under their pillow with a cheer-up note.
- Hang up pictures and decorations that make your home bright and cheerful.
- Find a nice music CD to play quietly in the background. There are so many good Christian artists whose songs really lift the soul. This is so much better than having a television on.
- Use your sweet smile to decorate your home! Walking around with a smile can really make others want to smile as well.
- Use kind words (remember we talked about this in *Modern and Modest?*). The Bible says that sweet words are like honeycombs. Fill your home with the honeycombs of your words.

*Always remember, when you serve others, you are really serving God!*

## Do it Anyway
### A poem by Mother Teresa

People are often unreasonable,
irrational, and self-centered.
Forgive them anyway.

If you are kind, people may accuse you of
selfish, ulterior motives.
Be kind anyway.

If you are successful, you will win some
unfaithful friends and some genuine enemies.
Succeed anyway.

If you are honest and sincere
people may deceive you.
Be honest and sincere anyway.

What you spend years creating,
others could destroy overnight.
Create anyway.

If you find serenity and happiness, some
may be jealous.
Be happy anyway.

The good you do today
will often be forgotten.
Do good anyway.

Give the best you have,
and it will never be enough.
Give your best anyway.

In the final analysis,
it is between you and God.
It was never between you and them anyway.

## *Have a Seat*

Posture is a part of your image, as well as your conversation and the way you dress. Let's say you have applied for a job and they call you for an interview. You want to make a good impression on your "future" boss. You make sure to dress appropriately for the occasion, great! Yet, at the interview, you sit across from your future boss leaning back in your chair, eyes wandering about the room. You are giving the impression that you are not interested in what she has to say, or in the job. If you were, you would sit straight or perhaps lean slightly forward in the chair, and look the interviewer in the eyes as she speaks.

See? Your body has a language that expresses what you think and feel. The way you stand, sit, cross your arms and move sends a message to the world.

### Here are a few rules of thumb:

- **For picking up something from the floor:** bend your knees, keeping them together. Never bend down with your back, as it's not good for your spine, besides, if you are wearing a skirt or dress, you will end up showing your undergarments!
- **Sitting on a chair:** It's appropriate for a young lady to keep her legs together or to cross one leg over the other, as long as it's done in a feminine way and doesn't show undergarments.
- **Standing straight:** Some teens slump. Slumping gives the impression that you don't feel very good about yourself or that you are trying to shrink or disappear. Even if you sometimes feel that way, try standing up straight. In the end, you really will feel more confident!
- **Getting in and out of a car, especially when wearing a skirt or a dress:** Open the car door, and slide one leg out of the car. Then swivel yourself getting your other leg out of the car and next to the first one. Get up and stand.

## *Going to See the King*

In medieval times, it was a wonderful privilege to stand in the presence of your king and render him honors. I bet you have read stories about this! Think about how people would prepare themselves to see the king. They would make sure to be clean and tidy and wear their best garments. There was a certain "protocol" or behavior that people needed to follow while in the presence of a King. For instance, as soon as people would enter the room where the king was, they were supposed to render the king honors by doing a curtsy. People were not supposed to eat in the presence of the king unless they were formally invited to eat with the king at the royal banquet. If you were offered a seat in the same room where the king was, it was very rude to cross you legs in his presence, and actually you could be taken out of the room just for doing that. Crossing your legs in front of the king meant that you had neither respect nor love for him.

Going to Holy Mass on Sundays, or at any time during the week, is a great privilege. Jesus waits for you in the Tabernacle. And, since He is the King of the Universe, you need to treat Him as such! You need to have special care in how you behave when you are in Church in the presence of the King.

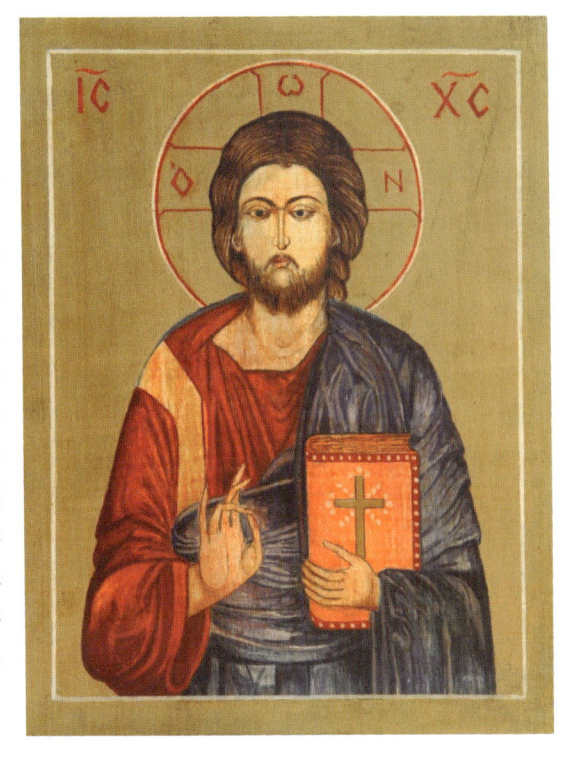

# Church Manners

### Hi Jesus, I'm here!
The very first thing you do when you enter a Church is find the Tabernacle and greet Jesus by doing a well-made genuflection. You do this by bending your right knee all the way to the ground, not half way! As you are genuflecting, don't forget to say in your heart "Hi Jesus, I'm here."

### In the presence of a King
Never cross your legs at Church. When people visit a king or a queen, for instance in Europe, they are reminded of this rule beforehand: Nobody crosses legs in the presence of a King. One of the reasons for this is that the soles of your shoes are dirty and to cross your legs reveals the dirty soles of your shoes to the king. And, Jesus is the King of Kings! Try crossing your ankles, instead. Remember to keep your legs together at your knees.

### An hour of fast
If you are old enough to receive Communion, you know about the Eucharistic fast. This means, not eating, chewing gum or drinking – except for water- a whole hour before receiving Jesus. This is a wonderful way to show Jesus that you really care and that you want to prepare yourself –body and soul- as best you can to receive Him.

### Love to chew gum?
Lots of people like to chew gum at all times of the day. Do you? Well, there are places and times where is appropriate to do so. Church is not one of them. This is one of the times where you can show Jesus how much you love Him by taking care of small details such as not chewing gum in His presence. Besides, when you are chewing gum before going to Communion, you are swallowing the "juices" that come from chewing the gum, and that breaks the Eucharistic fast, therefore you should not receive Our Lord.

### A good participant
Participate in the Mass! Do not just come to Mass acting as if you were dragging your body and can hardly stand up straight.

Remember, body language says a lot about you as a person. Jesus IS watching you. What do you want Him to see? It is important for you to realize that your efforts in honoring Him show Him you understand the respect He deserves. He died for you. The least you can do for Him is participate in Mass. It seems so miniscule when you think of it that way, doesn't it?

Once you realize that you are in the presence of the King of Kings, you'll want to stand straight, like a soldier for Christ. You'll want to be attentive and participate by singing and saying the prayers out loud. You'll sit straight on the pew without leaning back. Your eyes should be focused on the Mass and not wandering all over the place.

## The most amazing Guest

Let's say that the Pope is visiting your city and decides to come over to YOUR house for a visit. WOW! What a privilege! How would you prepare for such an important guest? I bet you would clean your house; perhaps your mom would put a beautiful flower arrangement in your living room to make the room more special. Your whole family would dress up to receive such an important guest. Once he arrived, you would give him all your attention, because you wouldn't want to miss even a minute of his visit, right? Well, in Communion, Jesus comes to you as a special guest to visit you. It's very important that after you receive Him you give Him all your attention. This is one of the most amazing moments of closeness that you can have with Jesus. Take advantage of this time to talk to Him about the things that make you happy, your worries; ask Him for His help in different things. Give Him thanks for the ways in which He takes care of you.

*It is by the conversion of the bread and wine into Christ's body and blood that Christ becomes present in this sacrament [Eucharist]. CCC #1375*

## Social Etiquette

Etiquette is another word for manners. Social etiquette refers to manners when being a hostess for a party or event. They are the manners you use when going to public places and even when receiving gifts. They are the ways to behave and be "social." See how "social" you are by taking the following quiz:

1. When you receive a gift, you write thank you cards for it.
   **Always          Sometimes          Never**
2. When a friend who is visiting you gets ready to leave your house, you see her to the door to say good bye.
   **Always          Sometimes          Never**
3. When you go to your friend's house, you greet her parents if they are around.
   **Always          Sometimes          Never**
4. If you see an older woman carrying a heavy grocery bag to her car, you offer to carry it for her.
   **Always          Sometimes          Never**
5. When getting in an elevator, you let people get off before you get on.
   **Always          Sometimes          Never**
6. You hold doors open for older people, parents carrying their children or people carrying packages.
   **Always          Sometimes          Never**
7. When guests come to your house, you stop what you are doing – computer, TV- to go to the door to greet them.
   **Always          Sometimes          Never**
8. You serve your guest a drink before getting one yourself.
   **Always          Sometimes          Never**
9. When you go to the movie theater, you place your trash in the garbage can instead of leaving it on your seat.
   **Always          Sometimes          Never**
10. When you get a ride to practice, you thank the driver.
    **Always          Sometimes          Never**

### Answer Key to Social Etiquette Quiz

If you answer mostly *Always:* Congratulations! You are Mannerly Mindy. You have great manners! You have a lot of confidence in yourself. Because you respect people, they respect you as well. Keep up the good work!

If you answer mostly *Sometimes:* You are Keep Trying Trudy. You are on the right track but can do better. Think about which areas in which you need the most improvement. Could it be in greeting others? Make a point to do better until you have mastered greeting others. Then find another area you can improve and do the same.

If you answer mostly *Never:* Face it you are a SLOB!!! You need to memorize this book!!! *But* it's never too late to start. The first step is to start thinking about others more, and less about you.

## *Etiquette Around the World*

Manners are different in different cultures. But remember, manners are an act of charity that make others comfortable. It's interesting to see how other country's etiquette is often similar or may be quite different. The important thing to remember is that as a daughter of the King you are always respectful to others, even if you don't understand why things are done certain ways.

Remember back in the beginning of the book, when we looked at the dignity of a person? Well, every country also has its own dignity. Actually, every country even has its own guardian angel! So respecting the country also respects the angel that God has given to it. And who doesn't want to respect a guardian angel?

When studying etiquette from around the world, you may even see things that your family does because they can be traced to your relatives' original country. If you never got around to making that family tree in *"Girls Rock!"* now may be the perfect time!

## *How to Get Along with the Brits*

- The British are reserved and polite.
- Protestants and Catholics do not mix socially.
- Handshakes are light, not firm, and everyone shakes hands, even children.
- Women extend their hands to men first.
- Always use titles such as, Doctor, Mr., Mrs., until you are invited to use their first names.
- While at dinner keep your hands on the table at all times, not in your lap.
- When the host folds his napkin, it is a signal that the meal is over.
- Always bring a small gift for the hostess of a party and she will open it right away.
- Never arrive at the stated time of the party, but 10-20 minutes late.

## *Hola Amigas*

- Mexico still has a class structure.
- Shake hands or bow when introduced.
- It is nice to bring flowers to the hostess of a party.
- Never show up on time for a party.
- When at dinner, always keep your hands on the table.
- Do not leave the table right after you eat. Mexicans like to visit at the table.
- Women like to look nice and always wear makeup.
- When in Mexico, the people appreciate any attempt to speak their language, Spanish.
- If you do not say good-bye, you will offend your hostess.

## *Japanese Manners*
- Japanese society is traditional and structured. They believe in loyalty, politeness, and personal responsibility.
- Handshakes are limp and people do not make eye contact.
- Always nod often when speaking with a Japanese person so that they know you are listening to them.
- Always be on time for a party or meeting.
- Any knowledge of Japanese history and culture are greatly appreciated.
- An empty glass or plate is a signal for more food. When you are finished eating or drinking, leave a little food on your plate and liquid in your glass.
- It is polite to try each dish served.
- Do not eat until the honored guest begins to eat.
- Always bring a gift for the hostess.

## *It's Greek to Me*
- Family is very important in Greece and the older people are very respected.
- Shake hands with everyone at a party when you arrive and when you leave.
- Always arrive 30 minutes late for a party.
- Eat everything on your plate.
- Greeks like to dance and to have their guests join in.
- Always bring a gift for the hostess.

## *Vive la France*
- The French are proud of their culture, history and language.
- Shake hands with everyone at a party.
- Family and friends greet each other with a kiss on both cheeks.
- Use titles until you are invited to use the person's first name. Only family and friends usually use first names.

- Always address people as Monsieur, Madame or Mademoiselle. Madame is used for all adult women over 18 years old.
- Do not comb your hair in public.
- Always be on time.
- Keep your hands on the table not in your lap.
- Never cut bread, tear it.
- Never eat fruit whole.
- Cross your knife over your fork if you want more food.
- Taste everything offered.
- Eat everything on your plate.
- Give a high quality gift to the hostess.
- Do not chew gum in public.

## Italy

- Italians are proud of their culture and family relationships are very important.
- Always shake hands with everyone present.
- Family and friends greet each other with a kiss on both cheeks.
- Use last names until you are invited to use first names.
- Always look people in the eye.
- Always be on time.
- Do not leave the table until all are finished eating.
- Roll the pasta with your fork not on your spoon.
- Use your knife to pick up pieces of cheese for your bread or cracker.
- Eat fruit with a knife.
- Wait for the hostess before you take a second helping.
- Bring a gift for the hostess and make sure it is wrapped beautifully.
- Never remove your shoes in public.

*Is your family's country not listed? Ask mom or dad to help you do some research and see what the proper etiquette from that country may be.*

# Visit Victorian Times

The late 1800's and early 1900's are called the Victorian era, after Queen Victoria of England. She had a large family and was a loving mother. It was said that being a mother was considered her most important role!

She is the one who coined the phrase, "We are not amused," which meant, *you'd better stop whatever you are doing because it's not a good thing!*

During this era, good manners and etiquette were very important. There were several books that could be read on this subject. Every young lady was taught how to walk, sit, stand, and eat. Read below and learn some of the things girls did and used in days gone by.

*Having good manners is never out-dated!*

## The Fan

Fans were a fashion accessory but were also used to communicate. The language of the fan was very intricate. Check out some of the fun fan facts:

- Fast fan-I am independent
- Slow fan-I am engaged
- Wide open fan-love
- Half open fan-friendship
- Shut fan-hate
- Twirling fan in right hand-I am watching you
- Fan behind the head-Don't forget me.
- Fan touching the left ear-Go away!

# The Autograph Book

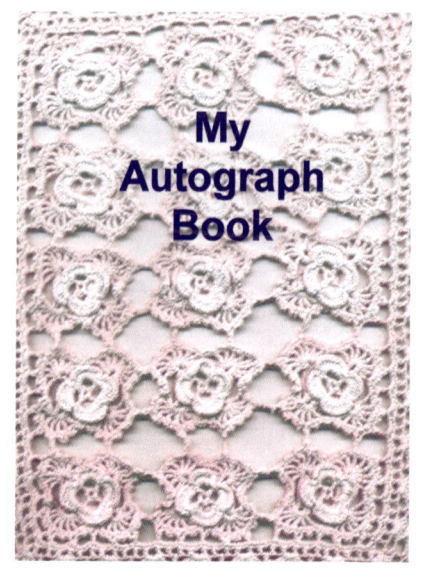

Girls would hand paint and decorate a special book called the autograph book. Girls would write thoughts, prayers, and poems in each other's books. Special teachers, family and acquaintances would also sign them and add something special to the page. Make your own book below.

**Materials:**
Cut card stock 4x6; Hole punch; Ribbon; Vellum-one sheet size of card stock; Embellishments such as glitter, lace, buttons, gems; Markers or Colored pencils

**Directions:**
Cut cardstock to size; Punch 3 holes on left side; Compile cardstock to make a book; Place Vellum on top and punch 3 holes; Tie ribbon through holes; Decorate book to your liking; Have people sign!

*If you are looking for something fun to do on a long, hot summer day or in the middle of a cold winter season, see if your mom will allow you to host an autograph book party. You can send invitations listing the supplies each girl will need. You can make it formal or informal and use the great info throughout this book for a smashingly fun time.*

## Calling Cards

Men and women used calling cards. These are like the business cards people use today only these were used for social reasons. They were printed by printers and were decorated with floral designs and calligraphy.

There was always a table near the front door with a silver tray where the guests would drop their card. Many etiquette rules applied for calling cards. Usually the lady of the house would have a certain day of the week to accept "callers," or guests. In those days there was a very structured social middle class and if you wanted to be in "society" you would try to get an invitation for lunch, or tea, by leaving your card at the house.

The use of cards, like the fan, had a language all it's own as well. The lady of the house could tell a lot about a person by his or her calling card.

- If the visitor came in person, the right upper corner was folded down.
- The visitor stopped to say "Congratulations" if the upper left corner was folded down.
- If the lower right corner was folded, the visitor was saying "Good-bye."
- A folded lower left corner meant, "I leave my sympathy."

You and your friends can make your own calling cards using cut card stock. Try it, it's fun!

*Mary Johnson*
*Daughter of the King*

## Flowers

As seen with fans and calling cards, flowers had a unique language. All these things were used in the Victorian times, which show the formality of society. Each flower or plant meant a certain thing.

- Calla lily-beauty
- Rose- love
- Violet-Faithfulness
- Baby's Breath-everlasting love
- Begonia-beware
- Carnation-affection
- Daffodil-respect
- Geranium-preference
- Iris-faith
- Lavender-devotion
- Orchid-love
- Tulip-charity
- Violet-modesty

Make a bouquet with a message and give it to someone you love.

## Scents

Bathing was only done once a week in Europe at this time. Hmmmm, it's no wonder the Victorians loved perfume and aromatherapy! Perfume was the counterfeit of real flowers.

Too much was in bad taste and not enough, well let's just say, deodorant was needed! Journals were kept with recipes for perfume and aromatherapy.

You may like to try these:

### Citrus-Mint Mist
Mix lemon and mint essential oils in a small glass bottle 6 drops per 1 cup of water. Shake and store in a dark place. Spray and smell!

### Lemon Cotton
Put a couple drops of lemon oil on a cotton ball and tuck it into your clothing drawer. All your things will smell fresh and clean.

# Tea Time

Plan a tea party with your friends and use your newly learned table manners. Victorian girls your age would've chosen this menu:

### Party Sandwiches

Use white bread and cut off crust. Spread bread with egg salad or chicken salad. If you are really feeling fancy, try watercress sandwiches. You have to remember that these sandwiches are meant to reflect your delicacy and they aren't supposed to be sub sandwiches. They are light and delicate.

Watercress has a sort of peppery taste and can even be used as a garnish because it is green and leafy. It usually comes in small bunches. Here's a simple, but elegant, recipe:

- *1/2 cup watercress*
- *1/4 cup parsley leaves, chopped*
- *1/4 cup butter, soft*
- *4 oz cup cream cheese*
- *2 tbs chives, chopped*

With an adult's supervision, cut up the watercress and parsley into small pieces. Mix them with the butter, cream cheese, and chives. Spread on bread. These can be served open-faced (only the bottom piece of bread) or as a sandwich in which you've put on a top piece of bread, as well. Either way, you should cut the sandwiches diagonally for a real Victorian treat. Place on pretty plate to serve.

### Fresh Fruit Plate

Choose in season fruits such as strawberries, blueberries, grapes, and melon. Cut into bite sized pieces. Serve in pretty glass bowl.

### Assorted Cookies and Scones

Make or buy your favorite cookies. Oatmeal cookies are easy to make and always yummy! If your mom or dad can take you to a bulk purchase store there are always great paper doilies to put on a plate that add a real flair to your presentation if you don't happen to have a decorative plate.

## Beverages

Tea of course! In a small bowl, place an assortment of tea bags. If you have a pretty little bowl for honey, put some honey out on the table with a little spoon of honey dripper for your guests to use. Most English tea drinkers put milk in their tea. That is a matter of opinion but it might be nice to have a small decanter of milk on the table, too.

With an adult's supervision or permission, bring a tea kettle of water just up to a gentle boil. Pour into cups for your guests. Never fill the cup with too much water and always be careful not to reach across anyone with something as dangerous as a pot of hot water.

Serving happens on a guest's right-hand side so stand to the right of each guest and bring her cup to you to pour and then gently, carefully place the cup back on the table in front of your guest. This is another reason that you shouldn't fill the cup too high. You want to enjoy the tea and not worry about spills.

If you don't care for tea, you can serve punch or sparkling water. A simple punch is to take your favorite variety of cranberry juice mixed with equal parts of unsweetened iced tea.

*Remember...
presentation is everything!
Use pretty dishes and napkins.
Be on your best behavior
and use your manners!*

## Virtues to Live by...

What is a virtue? Very simply, a virtue is a good habit that inclines you to do whatever is good. Virtuous behavior helps you live a good, happy life. But there is more to virtues than that. A single good action does not constitute a virtue. For instance, a person wouldn't be considered to have the virtue of generosity if she shared her candy with her friends only once. In order to become a virtue, a good habit has to be repeated on a regular basis.

## Kindness

Kindness is the act of being charitable towards other people. It's characterized by goodness, affection, gentleness, consideration and the disposition to help others. The world needs kindness! By being kind, you have the power to make the world a happier place to live. Kindness is inspired in your love for God: "You shall love the Lord your God with all your heart, with all your soul, with all your strength and with all your mind." When you love God with all your being, that love outpours into love for others; bitterness, sarcasm and meanness disappear. As Jesus has said, "Love your neighbor as yourself." When you are kind, you put others in the place of yourself and you treat them in the way you would like to be treated.

Kindness anticipates other's needs and wishes, for instance, you see your mom getting dinner ready and offer to set the table without her asking you. A little kindness goes a long way!

In order to be kind, you need to be sure your actions, words and thoughts are kind. You have read about kindness in actions and words already in this book. Thoughts are very important too. It's very hard to act kindly towards others, if you have unkind thoughts about them. Some examples of unkind thoughts are grudges, jealousies, envy, criticism, and feeling superior. So, in the same way you remove a weed from your garden by pulling the root out, you need to "root out" the unkind thoughts. One way to do this, is, any time you catch yourself thinking an unkind thought, you stop yourself right away and replace that thought with a kind one. Here is one example. You catch yourself thinking "Wendy shouldn't be in the basketball team...she is such a lousy player" Then you replace the unkind thought about Wendy for a kind thought: "Wendy is always such a good sport!"

### Possible goals to help you grow in kindness:

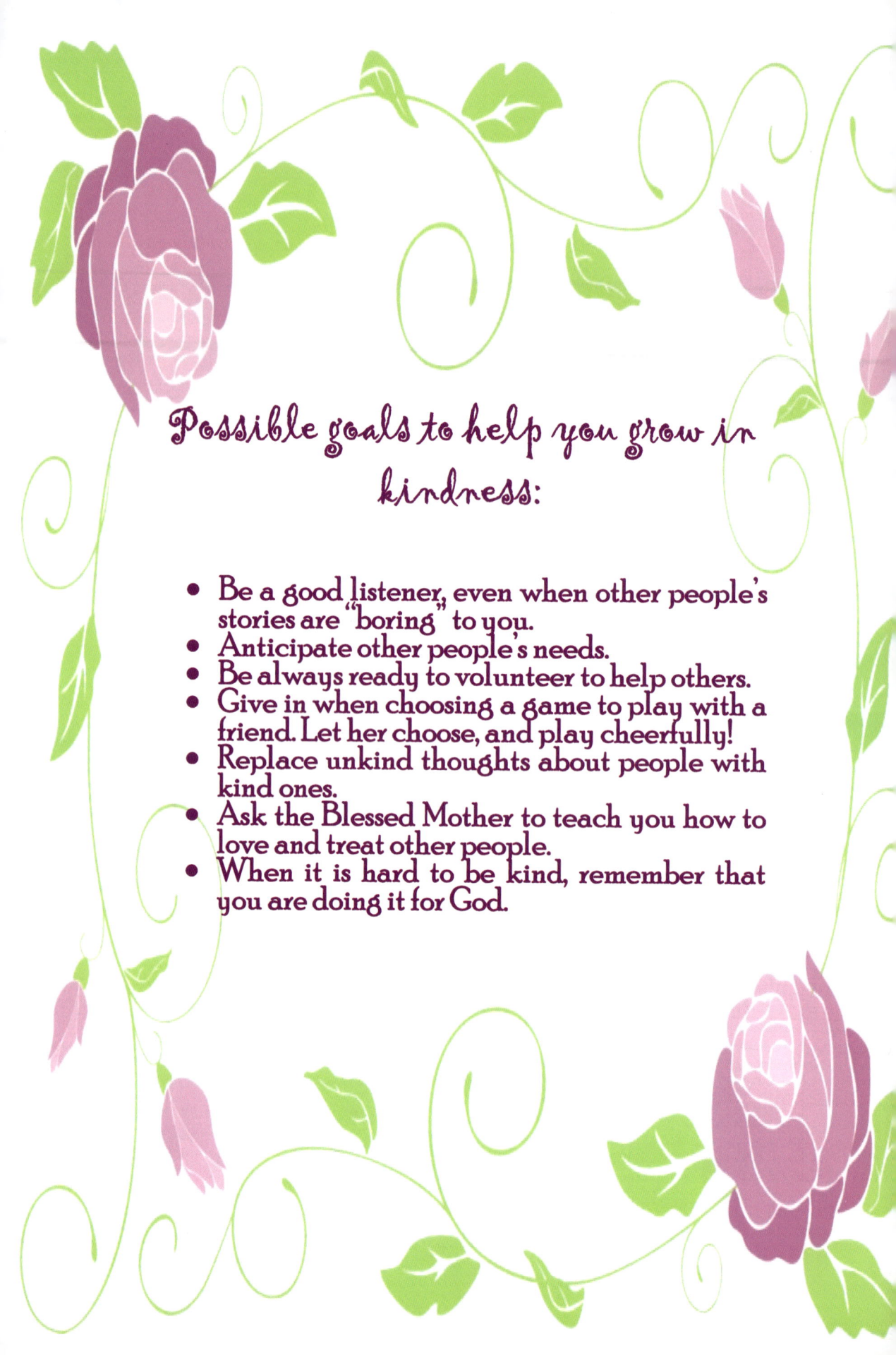

- Be a good listener, even when other people's stories are "boring" to you.
- Anticipate other people's needs.
- Be always ready to volunteer to help others.
- Give in when choosing a game to play with a friend. Let her choose, and play cheerfully!
- Replace unkind thoughts about people with kind ones.
- Ask the Blessed Mother to teach you how to love and treat other people.
- When it is hard to be kind, remember that you are doing it for God.

### Things to Think About

- Do I greet people with respect?
- Am I aware that when I serve others I am really serving God?
- Do I think about ways in which I can make life easier for my family members?
- Am I the heart of my home?
- Do I try to stop any unkind thoughts about people that come to my mind?
- Am I kind in my words? Do I use swear words?
- Do I keep the hour fast before receiving Jesus in Communion?
- Do I watch my posture at Church? Am I a soldier for Christ?
- When I go to Mass, Do I realize that I am in the presence of my King? Do I behave in a proper manner?
- Do I show others that I really care about them by having good manners when I am eating?

# YOU'VE GOTTA HAVE A PLAN!

You know it is important to take care of and control your body. In the same way, you need to take care of your soul. You need to nourish it so that it can grow in friendship with Jesus. How is that done? You gotta have a plan!

Do you think athletes make it to the Olympics by chance? Do you think they go with the flow and train here and there and somehow one day they end up in the Olympic games winning a medal? Of course not, you know that! They have a plan that includes diet and training. They follow it everyday, even when they don't feel like it. This dedication allows the athlete to attain their goal, their dream of winning a medal at the Olympics.

Think about the purpose of your life, to know, love and serve God in this life and to be happy with Him forever in the next. Do you think you can achieve this goal without some planning and preparation?

Here's a simple but effective plan you can use your entire life to complete your training here and attain your Heavenly goal. You can also use the special "All Things Girl" journal to write your own plan, prayers, and thoughts.

*Without me you can do nothing.*
*~John 15:5*

# *It's All Part of the Plan*

## WHAT THINGS SHOULD BE PART OF YOUR PLAN?

## MORNING OFFERING:

A good way to start your day is to say, "Hello, Jesus!" The day ahead is a great gift from God. The morning offering consists of giving Jesus everything you will do and say that day. Tell Him you want to please Him and give Him glory in all that you do.

You can make up your own special prayer or you can choose one to memorize. For example, here's a very simple prayer.

*"Good Morning dear Jesus this day is for you, I ask you to bless all that I say and do. Amen"*

Or

*"Oh Jesus through the Immaculate Heart of Mary I offer you the prayers, works, joys, and sufferings of this day, For all the intentions of Your Sacred Heart, in union with the Holy Sacrifice of the Mass said throughout the world today, in reparation for my sins, for the intentions of all our associates, and for the intentions of the Holy Father this month. Amen"*

It is important to try and say your morning offering at the same time every day so that you remember to do it. Some girls will say it right when they wake up. Others, when they sit down to breakfast. Whatever works for you, just do it!

## DAILY PRAYER. 
Prayer is talking to Jesus. It is something great! Jesus prayed and openly encouraged his disciples to pray. And guess what? You, as a daughter of the King, are a disciple. How does a person learn to pray? Start out by setting aside 5 minutes of your day to sit down in a quiet place where there will be no distractions. Place yourself in the presence of Jesus, asking your guardian angel to help you start a conversation with Jesus. Because prayer is an intimate conversation with God, you can talk to God as your best friend and tell Him the things that are concerning you, what is making you happy, angry or sad; God is always listening. You may tell Him something like: *"Hi Jesus, guess what I'm doing today? I'm going to my cousins' house! Mom said I have to clean my room before going....and you know Jesus, I hate cleaning my room! But I guess I'll do it.... Maybe I should offer it up for a special intention, eh? Who needs prayers, Jesus?....."* On you go. You are praying! Slowly

increase the 5 minutes of prayer a day to 10 minutes. You will feel so happy when you spend time talking to Jesus every day!

## THE ROSARY OF THE BLESSED MOTHER.

Do you enjoy looking at family pictures and remembering those precious moments? Well, when you pray the rosary you contemplate moments in the lives of Jesus and Mary on each mystery. The rosary is divided into 4 parts: each part into five mysteries. For each mystery one Our Father and Ten Hail Mary's are prayed while you meditate on a certain time of Jesus' life. The name rosary means "crown of roses". Think about each of the Hail Mary's you pray as a rose offered to Our Lady. By the end of the rosary, you have offered her a huge bouquet of beautiful roses! If saying the entire rosary seems like a big task, start out with just one decade and slowly add one at a time. The idea is to make the effort and to keep on trying.

## EXAMINATION OF CONSCIENCE AT NIGHT.

Before going to bed, it's a good idea to take a quick look at your day in God's presence to see if you have behaved as a daughter of the King. An easy way to do this is by asking yourself these three questions:

- *What did I do today that was pleasing to God?*
- *What did I do today that was not pleasing to God?*
- *What does God want me to do better tomorrow?*

Ponder briefly on each question, and then follow with an act of contrition to tell Jesus that you are sorry for having offended Him. An Act of Contrition is just a short prayer telling Jesus you are sorry for your sins. It can be as simple as *"I'm sorry, Lord. Help me do better tomorrow."* Or it can be the traditional Act of Contrition, *"Oh my God, I am heartily sorry for having offended thee and I detest all my sins because of the loss of Heaven and the pains of Hell, But most of all because they offend Thee my God who are all good and deserving of all my love. I firmly resolve with the help of Thy grace, to confess my sins, to do penance and to amend my life, Amen."*

## PRAY THREE HAIL MARY'S AT NIGHT BEFORE GOING TO BED ASKING THE BLESSED MOTHER TO HELP YOU KEEP YOUR HEART PURE.

Don't delay, start today, you can win the Olympics of the spiritual life!

## ST. FAUSTINA

# A GIRL LIKE ME!

St. Faustina was born Helena Kowalska in Glowgowiec, Poland August 25, 1905. She was the third of ten children. Her parents were considered peasants. Even as a child of seven, she felt the stirrings of a vocation to religious life. Helena loved work, prayer and obedience. She also had a heart for the poor. When she was nine years old, Helena received her first Holy Communion. She experienced profoundly the presence of Jesus in her soul. She went to school for only three years and then at the age of sixteen left home and went to work to help provide for the family. Helena longed to go into the convent, but her parents refused permission. They needed her to help support her family.

Helena worked as a housekeeper in two different towns. During this time, she continued to feel called to the religious life. After a dance one evening, Jesus appeared to her asking, "How long must I wait for you?" Helena applied to several different convents only to be turned down. She was finally accepted to the Congregation of the Sisters of Our Lady of Mercy. There she took the name Mary Faustina of the Blessed Sacrament.

Sr. Faustina's life appeared dull, and insignificant. Her jobs included cooking, gardening and being a porter. She always did her best and was kind and cheerful. Behind this apparent monotonous life, Faustina had a rich and extraordinary union with Jesus. She had a childlike trust in Him.

Despite Sr. Faustina's lack of education, she kept a diary. She wrote of all her experiences and special calling. She had devotion to the Blessed Sacrament and to the Blessed Mother. Sr. Faustina experienced gifts such as revelations, visions, and prophecy to name a few. She was also given the privilege of seeing the spiritual world of Purgatory and the Saints. Even with all these gifts, Faustina knew these would not make her holy. In her diary she wrote,

### NEITHER GRACES, NOR REVELATIONS, NOR RAPTURES, NOR GIFTS GRANTED TO A SOUL MAKE IT PERFECT, BUT RATHER THE INTIMATE UNION OF THE SOUL WITH GOD.

And so she strived to be perfect, holy like any other person.

Jesus chose Faustina for a special mission. He chose her even though she had very little education or talent for anything special. He asked her to be His Apostle of Mercy. He gave her three things to do. First, to remind the world about the Faith, and about God's love and mercy to every human person. She was then asked to beg for God's mercy for the whole world and individuals through the prayers, devotions and special Divine Mercy picture Jesus would give her. The third thing asked of Faustina was that she start an entire Movement of Divine Mercy.

With difficulty, Sr. Faustina did all that Jesus asked of her. She found an artist to paint a picture of Jesus with a ray of white light and a ray of red light coming from His heart and an inscription which said, "Jesus, I trust in You." When she saw the painting it made her sad. Jesus was so much more beautiful than the painting! How could a painting truly represent Jesus?

Sr. Faustina was given special prayers called the Divine Mercy Chaplet that she shared with the Faithful. The Sunday after Easter is now the Feast of Divine Mercy. If you go to confession seven days before or after this feast, with a real sincere wish to never sin

again, and go to Mass and receive Holy Communion, you will be forgiven all your sins and punishment due your sins will be taken away. This is how much Jesus wants to forgive sin and save souls! Today there are millions of religious, priests and lay people who pray the Divine Mercy Chaplet.

In 1936 Sr. Faustina became ill with tuberculosis and moved to a sanatorium. She kept her diary, offered her suffering for sinners and recited the Divine Mercy Chaplet. She died October 5, 1938 at the age of thirty-three.

Her diary left a story of her union with Jesus. Already in the years 1965-67, investigation into her life and holiness began. In 1968 her Beatification began in Rome. On April 18, 1992 Pope John Paul II raised Sr. Faustina to the glory of sainthood. She is now the saint known for showing the modern world God's Divine Mercy.

## THE DIVINE MERCY CHAPLET

1. Use your rosary beads to say the "Divine Mercy Chaplet."
2. Begin with the Sign of the Cross, 1 Our Father, 1 Hail Mary and The Apostles Creed.
3. Then on the Our Father Beads say the following: Eternal Father, I offer You the Body and Blood, Soul and Divinity of Your dearly beloved Son, Our Lord Jesus Christ, in atonement for our sins and those of the whole world.
4. On the 10 Hail Mary Beads say the following: For the sake of His sorrowful Passion, have mercy on us and on the whole world.
5. Repeat step 2 and 3 for all five decades.
6. Conclude by saying this three times: Holy God, Holy Mighty One, Holy Immortal One, have mercy on us and on the whole world.

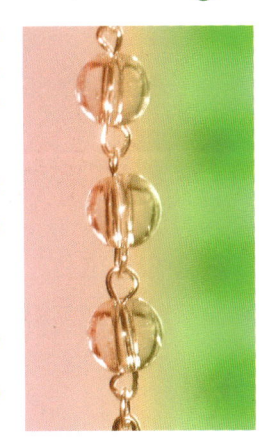

Printed in the United States
134900LV00001B